C.D. Howe

John D. Harbron

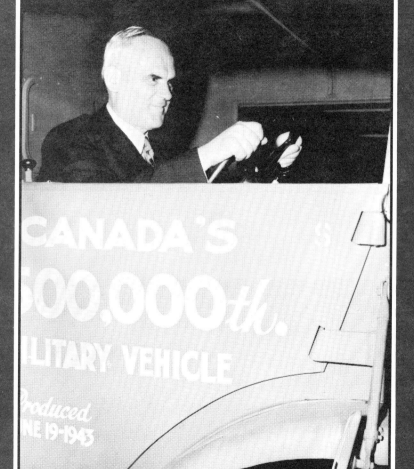

CANADA'S
500,000th.
MILITARY VEHICLE

Produced
JUNE 19-1943

Fitzhenry & Whiteside Limited

C.D. Howe

Contents

©1980 Fitzhenry and Whiteside Limited
150 Lesmill Road, Don Mills, Ontario M3B 2T5

Editors Diane Mew, Rosalind Sharpe
Designer Susan Budd

Printed and bound in Canada by
T.H. Best and Company, Don Mills, Ontario

The Canadians A continuing series
General Editor Robert Read
Series Editor Rosalind Sharpe
Consultant Editor Roderick Stewart

Harbron, John D., 1924-
   C.D. Howe

(The Canadians)

Bibliography: p. 64
ISBN 0-88902-226-7

1.   Howe, Clarence Decatur, 1886-1960.   2.
Statesmen — Canada — Biography.   3. Civil
engineers — Canada — Biography.   1. Series.

FC611.H69H37   971.0630924   C79-094431-6
F1034.3.H6H37

Minister of Everything

During the Second World War, when Canada was one of the leading Allied powers fighting against Nazi Germany, Fascist Italy and Imperial Japan, the most powerful man in Canada was neither a general nor an admiral, but a civilian with a stern face who always wore rumpled suits and wide-brimmed hats.

His name was Clarence Decatur Howe and he was the Minister of Munitions and Supply in Canada's wartime federal government. In that position he organized and controlled Canada's mammoth war effort, from which the country emerged as one of the world's leading industrial nations. But C. D. Howe was more than the politician who did the most to mobilize Canada for the most serious war in its history. Before the war he had modernized the nation's railways, airlines, ports, and radio system. And when the war ended, in 1945, he was in charge of converting this vast wartime production to the consumer needs of peacetime. No man in Canadian history before or since has controlled so many Canadian workers and executives, or helped to change our society so quickly.

Like many other important figures in Canada's past, C.D. Howe was born in the United States, and never lost his New England accent, even though he moved to Canada in 1908 and spent most of his life here. He had almost as many personal friends and associates among the big industrialists of the United States as he did in the Canadian business community, and he believed strongly in close links between the Canadian and American economies. He has been severely criticized for this. With the rise of economic nationalism in the 1960s and 1970s, and mounting pressure for Canadians to "buy back" their industries from the many American and foreign-owned branch plants operating in their country, C. D. Howe has emerged as some kind of villain who sold out Canada to the Yankees.

Nothing could be further from the truth. Howe was a loyal and devoted Canadian. When Canadian businessmen would not take up the challenge after World War II, he encouraged many existing foreign-owned companies in Canada to expand because he remembered the Great Depression of the thirties and the time after the First

World War, when companies closed as war work ceased and returning veterans could not find jobs.

Howe's true character is not easy to understand. He was not a politician in the open style of today, when we expect to know almost everything about the private lives and personal views of our leading public figures, and

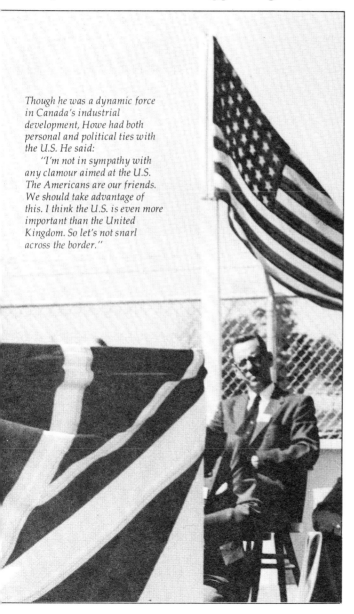

Though he was a dynamic force in Canada's industrial development, Howe had both personal and political ties with the U.S. He said:

"I'm not in sympathy with any clamour aimed at the U.S. The Americans are our friends. We should take advantage of this. I think the U.S. is even more important than the United Kingdom. So let's not snarl across the border."

when our political leaders appear nightly on the late-night television news. That was not Howe's style; indeed, when television was first used for political purposes, in the election of 1957, he was ill at ease with the cameras and his unsympathetic television image may have contributed to his defeat.

Howe was a very private person, more at home in the boardrooms of industry or among cabinet colleagues managing his large department of government, than with the public at large. He had little patience with the constant bickering and political rhetoric of Parliament. Over the years his irritation showed, and he gradually gained a reputation for being arrogant — a dictator who rode rough-shod over the Opposition and the public alike, drunk with power and ruthless in its use.

This is much too simple an assessment of a complex and fascinating man. The greatest legacy of C.D. Howe to Canada was his supreme confidence in its ability to become and remain one of the great industrial nations of the world. This American-born Canadian who always spoke with a Yankee twang was a man of his times, and his great accomplishments for Canada must be recognized in that context.

Boston Tech Chapter 2

Clarence Decatur Howe was born on January 15, 1886, in Waltham, Massachusetts, into a New England society whose nineteenth-century values and accomplishments remained unchallenged during his childhood and adolescence. The famous "Yankee ingenuity" which resulted in the design and production of navigational instruments, industrial machinery and modifications to the steam engine, took place mainly in the states of New

Clarence Howe as a baby in Grantham, Massachusetts, around 1886

England and impressed the young boy, who showed an early interest in mechanical devices.

The region was filled with small industrial towns surrounded by prosperous farming communities. In more and more sophisticated factories, the towns produced a growing number of modern conveniences such as stoves, compasses, watches, textiles and farm machinery. Howe's home town was the New England centre for watchmaking. The surrounding farms supplied food for a nation that was still expanding at around the turn of the century, long before the wheat-producing states of the West had been cultivated.

Howe's life-long values — a belief in hard work, thrift, honouring the privacy of the family — were those of a conservative, outwardly placid but competitive New England of the last century.

C.D. Howe's father, William, was one of nine children born into a comfortable middle-class New England home in 1849. He spent all his life, except for an eight-year spell in Colorado, in the state of Massachusetts, settling eventually in Waltham. When William returned from Colorado to his home state in 1883 he married Mary Emma Hastings of East Bethel, the daughter of a prosperous farmer and a teacher at the Bethel Academy.

The Howes were among the leading citizens of Waltham. William served as president of the town's board of aldermen and was a Republican Party legislator for a single term in the Massachusetts House of Representatives. By the time Clarence, their first child, was born, William was doing well in his carpentry and house-building business. The house on Stevens Street where Clarence was born was a pleasant one-and-a-half-storey bungalow built by William himself on a large plot of land, surrounded by a fruit and vegetable garden, with William's carpentry workshop conveniently situated at the back of the house.

A second child, Agnes, was born in 1889. She and Clarence got on well together, but as the only boy in the family, it soon became clear that Clarence would get preferential treatment when it came to education and training for a future career.

During his boyhood, young Clarence spent each summer at the farm homestead of his grandfather John

*William Howe, Clarence's
father*

Decatur Hastings. It was a fine farm, centred around a
large white farmhouse built during the American Civil
War. Clarence had been named Decatur after his
grandfather who, like many New Englanders of the
nineteenth century, had been given the name by
patriotic parents in remembrance of the American
seaman Stephen Decatur who defeated the "Barbary
pirates" from North Africa in 1806. He was one of the
first naval heroes of the young United States republic.

For Clarence, these summers were happy times, often
to be remembered in later life. Howe's nephew, describ-
ing his uncle at this time, recalls the scene:

Thus the young Clarence would come to know summers of swimming,
haying, sweet corn, dairy butter, raw milk, johnny cake and beans on
Saturday night. His uncle Fred Howe had married his mother's sister
Agnes and lived on the farm next door.

It was in this early idyllic setting that Howe would learn much of
his appreciation of rural life which would hold him in good stead
while building grain elevators in the Canadian West and much later in
selling that grain to the world.

Clarence and Agnes went to the local school. But, while most of his contemporaries left school at fourteen to go out to work, Clarence's parents saved to be able to send him to Waltham High School. For Mrs. Howe, this was to be the stepping stone from which her son would move on to study in Boston at the famous Massachusetts Institute of Technology (then known as the Boston Tech.)

Clarence worked hard at high school. Having been a teacher, his mother had impressed on him the value of learning; she encouraged in him a sense of purpose and a desire to make his mark in the world. He was not a brilliant student, but when he graduated in 1903 he dutifully set out for the grand city of Boston to write his entrance exams to Boston Tech. He passed, and in September 1903 entered the college to study civil engineering.

Howe was fortunate to be studying at what was, at that time, one of the world's leading centres of science and engineering. At the turn of the century American optimism in the future was unbounded. In this booming and expanding economy, businessmen and skilled engineers would be in great demand. The future for Howe looked rosy.

Once again he applied himself to his books, and was a favourite pupil of his professor, George Swain. He had always been fond of sports, especially baseball. At college he managed the college basketball team during his first two years, and even occasionally took time out to attend class parties, where he was popular with the local girls as a result of his excellent abilities as a dancer.

Following accepted tradition, undergraduates were expected to work in the summer holidays. Howe was fortunate to be apprenticed to the engineering firm of J.B. Worcester and Co. He worked as a draughtsman, and if the money he earned was useful, the experience was invaluable. Joseph Worcester had built the Boston subway system and was involved in the rebuilding of San Francisco following the devastating earthquake of 1906. Although Worcester had his office in Boston, the draughtsmen worked out of his house in Waltham. It was there that Clarence met Worcester's two daughters, one of whom was destined to become his wife.

After graduation in 1907, Professor Swain offered

*Clarence Howe with his sister
Agnes around 1890*

Howe a job as his teaching assistant. Howe accepted, although he was not entirely happy to stay at MIT, since his New England sense of ambition and desire to "get ahead" told him he should move elsewhere. Moreover, the United States in 1907 was entering the first of several twentieth century recessions. The twenty-one-year-old lecturer looked north to Canada, where in contrast an economic boom was under way, inspired by a wave of immigration and the development of the newly formed prairie provinces.

An opportunity to spread his wings arrived when Professor Swain was asked to recommend candidates for the new department of civil engineering planned for Dalhousie University in Halifax, already well known for its arts and law faculties.

According to the Howe family, Professor Swain suggested that Howe and his friend and fellow engineer James Barker toss a coin for the job. That is not how Barker remembers it. He was not interested in the job and anyway, according to Barker, no one at MIT would be foolish enough to toss a coin with Howe — he had a reputation for being uncannily lucky and his opponent would almost certainly lose.

Whichever way the decision was made, Howe was offered the job. With a starting salary of $2 000 a year, and an advance of $100 from the university to meet his expenses until his first pay cheque, Howe set out for Canada. His teaching career would be brief, but he was to spend the rest of his life in Canada.

New Horizons

The university to which the novice lecturer had come was small by present-day standards. The total enrollment was only about four hundred, and the teaching staff was very small, so Howe's lecturing duties were heavy. At twenty-three, he was hardly older than most of his students, but he soon managed to establish a good relationship with them. He, too, was learning, and he never hesitated to admit that he didn't have all the answers. On field trips with his students, it was a matter of tackling the problems together as they came along, the

In 1908 when he moved to Canada, C.D. Howe was a young man with a determined chin, a forthright stare and bright prospects. He spoke with a New England twang (calling Canada "Canader"), was popular, athletic and a good student. Armed with a degree in civil engineering and a lot of ambition, he was ready to make his mark in the world.

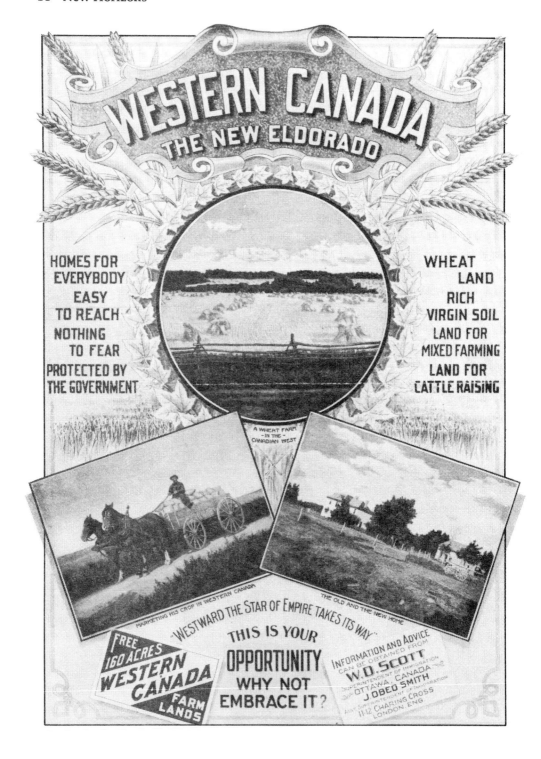

Howe theory being that there was nothing that could
not be solved by the application of common sense and
hard work. It was a theory that he would put into
practice in many other circumstances and at many other
times throughout his life.

The social life in Halifax was very pleasant. As a
member of a respected university — and a fancy-free
bachelor — there was no shortage of invitations and
social activities. His dancing ability made him a
favourite with the Halifax girls, and like the rest of the
citizens of Halifax, he enjoyed the water sports and
yacht-racing for which the city was famous.

Perhaps Howe would have settled down to a quiet,
respected but uneventful academic career, had it not
been for his friendship with one of his senior colleagues
at Dalhousie. Robert Magill was a professor of philosophy, who, because of his fairmindedness, had earned
himself a reputation as a skilled arbitrator, particularly
in labour disputes. When the Saskatchewan government
found trouble brewing between the local farmers and the
large grain companies who sold their wheat, they set up
a royal commission to look into the problem, headed by
Magill.

Magill came up with the obvious answer: in order to
have the power to negotiate with the grain companies,
the farmers should band together and go into the market
themselves. They followed this advice, and the federal
government set up the Board of Grain Commissioners to
supervise the grain business and help the farmers.
Inevitably, Magill was chosen as commission chairman.

All these events were of little concern to Howe, busy
with his engineering students. But the following year he
heard unexpectedly from his friend. Magill was now
established at Fort William, at the head of the Great
Lakes. There, the wheat brought in by train from across
the prairies was loaded on to ships for Montreal and
export abroad. Magill soon decided that the Board of
Grain Commissioners needed its own grain elevators
at the Lakehead to store surplus from one year to
another, and to grade and mix the wheat. The question
was, where to put the elevators, and how to get the most
up-to-date design. Magill remembered his young friend
back east in Halifax. He invited Howe to come to Fort
William to supervise the building of the elevators.

*The west attracted Howe: with
its largely unexploited resources,
it held potential fortunes for
those enterprising enough to take
up its challenges*

There was no hesitation on Howe's part; Halifax had little more to offer him, and it was time to move on. With typical Howe brevity, he replied: "I've never seen one of these things in my life. But I'll take the job."

So in the summer of 1913 Howe pulled up stakes again; but this time he was going to the raw frontier society of the Lakehead. At the same time he judged that he liked Canada enough to stay, and to throw in his lot with the young, developing nation. So he became a Canadian citizen.

Howe travelled west on the Canadian Pacific Railway through the bush and rock of the Canadian Shield. It was the railway that had built the wheat economy of the West. By 1912 the prairies were producing over six billion kilograms of wheat annually, and alongside the thin rails of steel stretching across the plains there appeared the now-familiar shape of the grain elevator. The grain trade made boom towns overnight. One of these was the twin city at the head of Lake Superior, Fort William and Port Arthur, where the grain was stored ready for sale and shipment to eastern Canada and an increasing overseas market.

Howe had arrived at the Lakehead at just the right time. The wheat boom was at its height, and the demand for storage capacity was increasing all across the West. After supervising the building of a large grain elevator at Port Arthur, the poorer sister town across the river from Fort William, Howe took a trip further west for the Grain Commissioners, overseeing the erection of elevators at Saskatoon, Moose Jaw, Calgary and Vancouver.

He was fascinated by the West — its spaces, its brashness, and its sense of limitless opportunity. His clients, the farmers, liked him. He was open to new ideas, straightforward in his approach, and down-to-earth in his attitude to technical difficulties.

In 1914 the First World War broke out in Europe, and by 1915 the demands for prairie wheat had risen, along with the price. In 1916 Canadian farmers produced over ten billion kilograms, and the Allied armies wanted even more.

Storage space for this flood of wheat was strained to the limit, and Howe saw his chance. His good relations with western farmers paid off, and he decided to set up his own engineering company to build grain elevators to meet this expanding need. In the summer of 1916 the C.D. Howe Company was formed.

Howe had taken the first step towards becoming a millionaire. In the time he had worked for the Board of Grain Commissioners he had lived frugally, as befitted someone of his New England background. Now, with his new enterprise underway and a little money in the bank, it was time to settle down. He was nearly thirty, and marriage seemed a sensible move. He remembered the daughter of his old boss, J.B. Worcester. In the fall of 1915 Howe travelled to Boston to pay court to Alice Worcester. After some surprise at a proposal of marriage from a young man she hardly knew, Alice decided that

Howe's grandfather and namesake, John Decatur Hastings, and his grandmother, Emma Hastings, sit in front of their farmhouse, where the young Clarence spent many summers. Howe is standing between his grandparents, with his mother seated at the right of the picture with his sister Agnes.

Howe was primarily a businessman, not a politician. He did not relish political intrigue and parliamentary negotiation for their own sakes; for him, Parliament, and political power, were means to an end — the end being to run the sectors of Canadian government which were his responsibility as efficiently and economically as possible. "Parliament got in his way" observed one critic; but charges that Howe's main objective was personal power were probably unfair.

Clarence Howe was a sober, hard-working man who was going places. To a girl of her generation and background, he seemed good matrimonial material. She accepted his offer and they were married the following September.

It was to be a long and happy marriage. The couple settled in Port Arthur, where Howe was on the way to becoming a respected and affluent member of the community. By 1923 they had moved into a substantial three-storey house overlooking the lake, and their five children were born there into the security of a warm family atmosphere. The children saw little of their father in those early years, however. In accordance with the rigid customs of the day, Howe left all domestic matters to Alice and did not interfere in the day-to-day running of the household — any more than he would have expected her to interfere in the running of his business.

He was a kind but rather distant father, hardly ever taking much part in the various activities of his children. Nevertheless, Howe was always a very domestic person. All his life he maintained a strict division between his private and his public life — a characteristic that had several advantages, one of which was that he never brought his business problems home with him.

In those early years the C.D. Howe Company certainly had its share of problems. The first contract they undertook was for the Saskatchewan Cooperative Elevator Company. Howe decided to build the elevator at Port Arthur. The neighbouring Fort William waterfront was crowded and the little available land was expensive. On the other hand, the waterfront at Port Arthur was low-lying and marshy, and not thought suitable to support such a massive structure. Howe inspected the site and thought otherwise: he committed himself to having the elevator built in time for the 1917 harvest.

At first all went well and on schedule. But Howe had not taken the weather into his calculations. On December 18, 1916, a gale swept across the lake, causing huge waves to smash into the wooden scaffolding and machinery. The site was a disaster; the infant company's finances had taken a blow from which few expected it to recover.

On inspection, however Howe discovered that the foundations were still intact. The town of Port Arthur rallied round — not least because of the cries of "I told you so" from their rivals across the river at Fort William. The breakwater was repaired, the local bank manager advanced Howe money to carry on his business, and when the ice went out of the bay in the spring, Howe brought in three hundred workmen to keep construction going round the clock, six days a week. By October 1917 the outside concrete structure was finished, and grain was being unloaded into the elevator by the new year. Not only was the C.D. Howe Company saved; its reputation was made. Howe became known as something of a miracle worker, and contracts poured in. With the further expansion of the economy after the end of the war, his fortune seemed assured.

The decade of the 1920s were good years for the C.D. Howe Company. From his office on the seventh floor of

By the early thirties Howe was already a millionaire as a result of his successful elevator construction business. He had also invented the Howe Dumper, a machine which could lift and empty a grain car in eight minutes. The Howe Company operated on an international scale: in 1931 for example, it built 300 grain elevators, costing $40 million, in Argentina, a country which continues to compete with Canada as a grain-exporting nation. Time magazine estimated that at the time of his death, Howe was worth $30 million.

the imposing new office block, the Whalen Building, Howe could look out to the grain elevators standing majestically on the waterfront. His company was responsible for building many of them; in 1926 it was reported that the firm had "designed and supervised the construction of industrial plants valued at over $30 million." Soon the company was acting as engineering consultant across the country, from Prince Rupert, British Columbia, to Churchill, Manitoba, or Prescott on the St. Lawrence River. By the end of the period, it had built grain elevators with storage space for one thousand million kilograms of wheat, the biggest one at Port Arthur holding almost two hundred million kilograms.

This good fortune was not to last. All through the 1920s the price of wheat was high, sometimes as much as seven cents a kilogram. But by 1929 the market was glutted. Canadian wheat had been in demand in Europe immediately after the war. But by now, most European countries had recovered from the ravages of war and their domestic grain production had been restored. Before long more grain was being produced in Canada than could be sold, and it had to be held in elevators from one year to another. Inevitably the price dropped, from four cents a kilogram at the end of the 1920s to a low of one cent in 1932.

With the onset of the Depression and the collapse of the grain industry, Howe's business began to fall apart. A staff of 175 in 1928 had shrunk to 5 by 1933. Finally, on New Year's day, 1934, Howe went to his office to find a letter of resignation from Ralph Chandler, his one remaining partner. It was the end of Howe's career as an engineer. The company would revive and prosper for many years, but not with Howe at its head. By that time he had moved into an entirely different line of work.

The Crown Corporations Chapter 4

Howe, as a young cabinet minister in 1936, signed this personal photograph for Prime Minister King

During the 1920s C.D. Howe's business had taken him to all parts of the country, including trips to Ottawa to consult with the government on engineering contracts. He made the acquaintance of both Conservative and Liberal politicians, but realized that if he wanted to preserve his business contacts no matter which party was in power, it did not pay to take sides too openly.

However, he could not fail to be aware of the impact the Depression was having, particularly on the West; nor was he any more happy than the rest of the country with the obviously inadequate policies of the Conservative government to solve these problems. Prime Minister R.B. Bennett was fast losing support, in spite of his "New Deal" social welfare policies, and by the end of 1934, the Liberal party was preparing for an election and what it confidently expected would be a crushing defeat for the Conservative government.

When a political party scents victory, as did the Liberals under their leader Mackenzie King in 1934, it starts to recruit likely-looking candidates. King realized the problems the nation faced were enormous — after all, the United States was also in the grip of this terrible Depression, and its economic health had a great effect on Canada — and that his own popularity would be short-lived if he did not provide some better policies than the Conservatives. King wanted some fresh faces in his future government. So he asked the Liberal party organizers to find candidates who would bring vitality, stability and new ideas to the running of the country.

C.D. Howe was just the type of candidate the Liberals were looking for. With the bottom dropping out of the grain market, it didn't take Mackenzie King's friends long to persuade Howe to allow himself to be nominated as Liberal candidate for Port Arthur. Although he was unknown in the world of politics and had few support-ers among long-time Liberals or the labour unions, Clarence and Alice Howe were prominent and respected members of the community at the Lakehead. When the election came in October 1935, Howe was able to remind the voters of the business he and his company had brought to their city. He was just the kind of man the electorate needed to represent them in Ottawa. In the great Liberal victory, C.D. Howe was swept into the House of Commons — an experienced businessman at the Lakehead, but a new boy in Parliament.

The Liberal sweep was overwhelming: 174 Liberal members were elected, to be opposed by only 40 Conservatives and a mere 7 of the newly formed socialist party, the CCF. Prime Minister King had campaigned on the slogan "King or Chaos," and he now turned his attention to selecting a cabinet that would provide the

country with stable leadership and vigorous policies and men. One of these men was C.D. Howe — who indeed was so new to the general public that for months after his election the Toronto *Globe and Mail* continued to refer to him as "Charles D. Howe."

Prime Minister Bennett, surrounded by members of his cabinet, speaks over the transatlantic telephone at the British Empire Trade Fair held at Buenos Aires in 1931.

Unlike most of Mackenzie King's cabinet, Howe really did represent a new kind of politician. For one thing he was an engineer — the only one in a cabinet composed of lawyers, farmers and a lone journalist. For another, he had had no previous involvement with Liberal party politics, and came to Ottawa as his own man, with no political debts to repay. He was still a comparatively wealthy man, and was one of the few men in the cabinet with any business experience. Howe represented the new blood King was looking for, so he found himself minister in charge of two departments, Marine and Railways.

The Ottawa to which the Howe family now moved certainly considered itself rather more sophisticated than the northern Ontario outpost of Port Arthur. Yet as a capital city it left something to be desired. The most prominent industry — after government and the civil service — was the pulp, paper and lumber business. The E.B. Eddy Company's pulpmills, in all their evil-smelling glory, were situated on the Ottawa River directly below the Parliament Buildings. The city itself had an enclosed, small-town feeling; everything revolved around the politicians and government departments clustered around Parliament Hill.

Alice and Clarence bought a home in the exclusive Rockcliffe area. It was an imposing house, overlooking the Ottawa River, with a large garden, suitable for a family of five growing children. For all his time in Ottawa this home, and Alice and the family, were to be a quiet refuge from the stresses and and tensions of the country's business. As James Oastler of the Montreal *Star* wrote in 1960 after Howe's death:

When he could get home at night, especially in the winter, the two would sit down in front of the fire; the minister would relax with his tea and ginger bread before retiring. His home was apart from his career. Here was his haven.

When Mackenzie King formed his third government in 1935 (he had previously been elected in 1921 and 1926), C.D. Howe, a newcomer to Parliament, was appointed cabinet minister responsible for Marine and Railways. Prime Minister King is seated at the centre of the picture, with Howe standing at back left. Howe, noted for his rumpled suits, was immaculately turned out in a morning suit complete with wing collar on this occasion.

C.D. Howe, the politician-executive who perhaps knew how to delegate authority more successfully than any cabinet minister before or since, left his work at the office at the end of the working day. "I have had enough for today, the rest can wait until tomorrow," he often said, even during the difficult war years. And he usually made it to bed by ten.

This was the pattern set early in the Howes' life. Little did either Clarence or Alice realize then that that house at Rockcliffe would be their home for over twenty years — during which period he was to become one of the most powerful men in the country.

Twenty-one years after his first appearance in the House of Commons in 1935, Howe sternly reminded a parliamentary heckler, "I have been working on sizable projects all my life. And somehow I reach a point in the development of a project where I begin to think it is important. And if it is a serious enough project, then I begin to think it is the most important thing in the world."

"Sizable projects" to bring Canada out of the economic slump of the Depression were the kind of thing Prime Minister King and his new cabinet had in mind for the country in late 1935. Howe's first task as a man who thought big was modernization of that vital sector on which Canada's prosperity at large rises or falls — the national transportation system.

First in line for Howe's attention were Canada's ports and harbours. By 1935 they were in a shocking state, badly run, and falling to pieces for lack of money for repairs. Most important, they were ideal means for dispensing patronage: in other words, jobs were given for political services. That meant that every time the government changed, one lot of inefficient employees was turned out of office, only to be replaced by another lot, equally inefficient, whose only recommendation was that they were friends of the party in power. That was no way to run a large communications network — or, indeed, any organization that had so important a part to play in the nation's trade.

The previous Conservative government had appointed a royal commission to look into the harbour crisis. It had recommended the formation of a central federal harbours board, safe from the temptations of

One of Howe's few personal friends, C.J. Mackenzie, later president of the National Research Council, recalled Howe's style of management: 'He had a keen sense of concentration. He read documents slowly but read them only once. He didn't put experts on the witness stand... he hired people he trusted. 'What are your instructions?' they would ask. 'I have no instructions, only responsibilities,' Howe would reply, 'and I want you to fulfill them.' "

government patronage. But the Tories were defeated before they could bring in the necessary legislation to make the changes.

Howe agreed with the recommendations — not surprisingly, since he had been one of the expert witnesses who had given advice to the royal commission. Within a few months of taking office he had prepared his own legislation creating a National Harbours Board to run many of the harbours and ports for the country.

When Howe presented his bill to the House of Commons in March 1936, he innocently assumed that no one could find anything to object to in such a reasonable proposal. The bill's reception was an eye-opener for him. Even members of his own party were unhappy at losing their opportunities to hand out patronage to their political friends (many of whom had been promised something for their help in the recent election campaign). The Opposition, though few in number, made up for it in noise. They subjected the clauses of the bill to detailed argument day after day. Above all they objected to the centralized control that would put so much power into the hands of the Minister of Marine — that is, C.D. Howe. This was the first faint echo of a theme that would be heard with increasing frequency in the years to come.

During this first of many future attacks in the House of Commons, Howe's impatience with parliamentary procedure also showed itself for the first time. He said:

. . . if my intentions had not been along the lines the Opposition is now advocating, I would not have brought this Bill to the point it has now reached. I must say I am getting a bit fed up with it and my resistance is getting to a low ebb.

Howe also experienced the first of many personal jibes the Conservatives would toss at him over the next two decades, when R.B. Bennett, then Opposition Leader, snarled at him: "The minister will soon learn Parliament is no drafting room."

Nevertheless, the passage of the National Harbours Bill represented the kind of action Mackenzie King anticipated from his tough new minister. He showed his pleasure by merging the two ministries of Marine and Railways into the important Department of Transport, with Howe as its minister.

While Howe was reorganizing Canada's harbours, he was also doing battle with the problems of the transcontinental railway system. By the 1930s Canada's railways were a shambles. Most of them were operated by the Canadian National Railways (CNR) which had been formed in the early 1920s from a merger of several bankrupt trans-continental railway lines built during the boom of the early twentieth century. Around that time an often-told joke about railway expansion in this country had it that "the British and Americans build railways for business, the Germans for war, and the Canadians for fun."

There was nothing funny about the debt-ridden CNR and the depressed privately owned Canadian Pacific Railway (CPR) by this time. Their equipment was run down and worn out. The so-called colonial coaches — those highly uncomfortable passenger cars which had brought European immigrants to the Canadian West at

This is one of the few pictures in which Howe does not appear surrounded by business or political colleagues in pin-stripe suits. Howe is standing with a group of chiefs of the Blood Indian tribe on the Blood reserve near Fort Alberta. Unlike many more publicity-conscious politicians, Howe refused to don an Indian head-dress for the picture.

the turn of the century and carried troops the other way to the war in Europe between 1914 and 1918 — were still in service. The farmers who were the mainstay of the railways were broke — ruined by both the Depression and by the terrible droughts of the 1930s. By 1934 grain exports were down to a trickle.

The object of Howe's immediate attention was the CNR. This had been formed under a previous Conservative government and public money had been pumped into it to save the line.

When the Liberals came into power in 1923 they appointed an American railway expert, Sir Henry Thornton, to take charge of the ailing railway. He had lavish ideas: the way out, in his view, was to spend money to attract business and compete with the CPR. Under his rule the CNR expanded its interests; it bought hotels, ran a fleet of cruise ships and steamers, and Thornton built himself a fancy official residence in Montreal. For a while the policy seemed to work. But the CNR still had massive debts left from the past, and when the Depression hit, all those dreams of solvency sank along with the price of wheat.

Sir Henry bore the brunt of the criticism; he was fired and the government appointed a three-man board to run the railway. It was an unfortunate decision. As Howe himself said when he came to clean up the mess, the board members "were laymen inexperienced in railway problems who knew nothing of actual railway practice," and they were responsible to no one.

Howe proposed to make the CNR a government-owned organization under a president and board of directors who would be responsible for the running of the railway, with authority to raise money to end its deficit. They would report to Parliament through the Minister of Transport — who was, of course, C.D. Howe. Once again, the charge of Howe's excessive appetite for power was raised by the Opposition. But Howe's proposals made good business sense, and there was really no alternative to a problem that had haunted successive governments for years. So the legislation to set up the board was passed in June 1936 and the structure that Howe created then largely exists to this day.

Howe's broad plan to change our communications systems included the existing radio services which, like

Howe, in 1942, delivers a pep-talk to workers in Sudbury, Ontario, a town producing nickel for wartime ammunition.

the troubled railways and harbours, had received much attention from the previous government. Another Tory royal commission had recommended the formation of a national radio service, which they had initiated as the Canadian Radio Broadcasting Commission. But it was a limited national radio agency drawing licence fees from radio set owners. There were only eight radio stations, seven of them in Ontario and Quebec. Moreover, the agency was closely associated with the financially shaky private radio stations.

Howe's answer again was to set up a government-owned agency — what we now know as a crown corporation. In June 1936, a bill to create the Canadian Broadcasting Corporation was passed without much discussion or opposition in the House. This bill provided for broadcast coverage for the whole country and gave the CBC control over both public and private broadcasting. The agency was modelled on the highly successful British Broadcasting Corporation. The corporation which Howe brought into being in 1936 has served Canada well ever since, in spite of the many technological changes that have taken place in the broadcasting industry since that time.

It was now time for Howe to try his hand at harnessing what in 1936 was still considered to be a brand new and exciting technology — air transport.

Air Canada Chapter 5

In the early evening of July 30, 1937, a twin-engine
Lockheed 14H of the Department of Transport touched
down at Vancouver's Sea Island Airport. Smiling
broadly, C.D. Howe came down the steps, followed by
his department officials and the pilot, who all looked
distinctly shaky and greatly relieved. It was the end of a
dawn-to-dusk flight from Montreal to Vancouver — the
first transcontinental flight ever made in Canada. It had
taken seventeen hours and thirty-four minutes.

This was Howe's way of marking the opening of the
new air age in Canada and the unofficial inauguration of
his new creation, Trans-Canada Airlines.

Used as we are to transcontinental flights aboard
gleaming 747s, it is difficult to grasp just how rugged it
was to fly across the country less than fifty years ago.
Such an adventure was only for stout hearts and even
stouter stomachs. Howe possessed both, and he had
great need of them that July day. He and his little band of
officials had left Montreal in a thunderstorm, after the
pilot, J.H. Tudhope, had been ordered to take the aircraft
out of its hangar against his better judgment. They made
the first refuelling stop at North Bay, but had to fly over
the next scheduled stop at Kapuskasing because of heavy
cloud, and hope to reach Sioux Lookout, the next
refuelling point. The TCA president later described the
incident:

> Tudhope was on his knees most of the time with the map, trying to
> figure out where they were, and just as they were out of gas they
> found themselves squarely on top of Sioux Lookout. Tudhope was a
> very relieved man.
> . . . It was a very fine piece of dead reckoning and very few men in
> Canada could have done it; on the other hand . . . there was a very
> large share of unadulterated good luck, because when one is flying
> without a beam and cannot see the ground, it is quite impossible to
> make correct allowances for wind drift.

They put down again at Winnipeg and then flew to
Vancouver over (or almost through) the Rockies at 3 500
metres, the plane's maximum altitude.

The publicity surrounding this episode was enormous, and Howe's faith in what he always called "his
airline" was to be fully justified. He had worked hard to

On the eve of their historic
"dawn-to-dusk" flight across
Canada on July 30, 1937, Howe
is pictured with the officials and
crew who accompanied him. The
chief pilot, Squadron Leader J. H.
Tudhope (with pipe) stands on
Howe's left.

bring it into existence. When Howe became Minister of
Transport in the 1930s, commercial air transport in
Canada was largely in the hands of bush pilots and their
small companies. Many of them were famous because of
their exploits during the First World War as fighter
pilots on the Western Front. But their peacetime
activities as civilian pilots of still fragile airplanes seemed
to show more bravado than business skill.

There were few commercial flights in Canada at the
time, and only one company of any significance,
Canadian Airways, which had taken over a number of
smaller operations. When the new Liberal government
came to power, it realized something would have to be
done quickly about air travel in Canada. In the United
States commercial airlines were already big business,
and many Canadians were getting into the habit of
journeying south of the border to take the U.S.
continental flights. If Canada was to have its own
transcontinental air service, rather than just providing

*After their harrowing trip Howe
appears relaxed, while his
companion H. J. Symington, a
director of Trans-Canada
Airlines (also seated), looks
rather distracted after the ordeal.
They were welcomed by the
Mayor of Vancouver.*

local feeder flights to connect with American airlines, clearly the government would have to supply the leadership. Howe was also determined to avoid the mistakes made in the past that had given Canada two competing, and often broke, transcontinental railways. There would be only one airline, and that would be under public control.

However, Liberal philosophy dictated that governments should not saddle themselves with large business operations which, in a free enterprise system, could be better run by private industry. In 1936 only socialists and communists advocated government ownership of all means of transportation. So the Liberals decided to create a company to run the airline whose capital would come from private transport organizations — in this case the two railway companies, the CNR and the CPR. Government would have representation on the board of management, would provide some of the equipment, such as airport facilities, navigational aids and so on, but would not be involved in the day-to-day running of the airline.

The CP management declined to be associated with the project; they regarded the CNR as being in effect the same as the government because of C.D. Howe's recent reorganization of its management, and they didn't see why CP shareholders should put their money into what they considered would become a "politically directed" corporation. So in the end, the money was put up by the CNR, whose president also became president of the new airline, and Trans-Canada Airlines came into being in March 1937.

In passing, it might be noted that CP did go into the airline business in 1942. They founded Canadian Pacific, and have complained ever since of unfair competition from Air Canada.

Trans-Canada Airlines (later renamed Air Canada) was to be the model for many other crown corporations that Howe would create during the war. Trans-Canada started scheduled operations in September 1937, and has continued to expand ever since. It was set up just in time. Already war clouds were gathering, and once again Canada's young men and women would be called upon to fight for democracy in Europe.

Dictator Howe Chapter 6

On April 9, 1940, only seven months after the Second
World War broke out, C.D. Howe was chosen by Prime
Minister King for the largest single job of his career. On
that day he became Minister of Munitions and Supply,
the new government department formed to steer Canada
into full war production. The organization of the
department (usually known as DMS) was a task which
remains unparalleled in our history, involving government, private industry and the entire work force of the
country. Its mandate was no less than the total
mobilization of all Canadian resources to fight the war.

But was Canada ready for such a big task? In the fall
of 1939 it was still recovering from the Depression, with
many factories still closed, high unemployment and
virtually no national training programs for the technicians required.

Canadians during the 1930s had been united by a
common grinding and negative bond, surviving the
Depression. Now, during the war, they would be united
by abhorrence of Hitler's Nazi doctrines, and loyalty to
the Europe now under attack. But there was much to be
done. The federal government was small, stingy from
saving money during the Depression, and without much
sense of vision for the monumental events ahead. The
Canadian armed forces were tiny, incapable of a
sustained defence role and certainly far from ready to
take part in another large European war. The country
itself, though dotted with emerging industries, was
basically agricultural. The average Canadian in that
eventful fall of 1939 was more easily identified as a
farmer, a coal miner or a lumberjack than a skilled
artisan or factory worker.

And yet within eighteen months of the outbreak of
war, this country had been galvanized into action. Farm
boys and girls and unemployed city youths either joined
the forces to become aircraftsmen, infantrymen, sailors
or tank operators, or flooded into the expanding war
plants to build corvettes for the navy, army trucks, tanks,
weapons, aircraft and all kinds of ammunition.

During the war Canada built 800 000 military transport vehicles, 50 000 armoured carriers, 300 corvettes (small ships specially designed for anti-submarine warfare) and minesweepers, millions of rounds of ammunition and thousands of tonnes of explosives.

LAUNCH OF
H.M.C.S. NOOTKA
SECOND TRIBAL DESTROYER
BUILT IN CANADA BY
HALIFAX SHIPYARDS LIMITED
HALIFAX NOVA SCOTIA

The official history of DMS makes the astonishing statement that "... by the end of 1943 there was hardly a factory or even a machine shop with more than a dozen employees that was not directly or indirectly engaged in war work." In one way or another they all relied on DMS for allocation of raw material, wartime markets, production volume and even skilled manpower. And without exaggeration, it can be said that most of the management that brought about that vast change to wartime production was the result of the aggressive organizing ability and quick mind of C.D. Howe as Minister of Munitions and Supply.

The Royal Tour of 1939 was a great success. Here King George VI and Queen Elizabeth leave the Houses of Parliament in Ottawa. Prime Minister Mackenzie King stands to attention at left.

The "new boy" who had first come to Ottawa just four short years before had come a long way. Broadcaster Norman Depoe summed up Howe's influence:

His impact would have been formidable in any capital at any time. In timid, stuffy, small-town Ottawa, still hag-ridden by depression nightmares, still proper and circumspect and a trifle pompous, he had something of the effect of a tidal wave.

How did this dynamic personality set about managing this vast national war effort? Mainly by appealing to

Howe was an admirer of Max Aitken, Lord Beaverbrook, shown here seated before his own portrait. Born in Newcastle, New Brunswick, Aitken turned a tiny insurance business into an immense financial empire in just seven years. Travelling to England, he gained a seat in Parliament and a baronetcy, and became a member of Churchill's wartime cabinet.

the patriotic instincts of Canada's senior executives and encouraging them to serve directly in the DMS or in government as the so-called "dollar-a-year men." These were men who continued to be paid by their firms during the war, but were on loan to the government for the war's duration at a token dollar a year.

The list of senior Canadian industrialists who answered Howe's call between 1940 and 1945 represented the cream of the country's top management, except for those Howe felt could serve the war effort better by managing their own plants. All of them were handpicked for their skills in decision-making, organization and making money. Among Howe's choices were H.R. MacMillan, British Columbia's postwar pulp and paper tycoon; W.C. Woodward, whose Vancouver department store expanded into a western Canadian chain in the 1960s; the distinguished Toronto lawyer Henry Borden, who would be president of Brazilian Light and Power, Canada's largest company doing business with Latin America; and that most famous of tycoons, E.P. Taylor, who after the war built the Toronto suburb of Don Mills, and had investments in breweries, real estate and race horses.

The War Committee of the Canadian Cabinet, 1943

Seated, left to right: Hon. C. G. Power; Hon. T. A. Crerar; Rt. Hon. Mackenzie King; Hon. J. L. Ralston; Hon. J. L. Ilsley. Standing, left to right: Hon. A. L. Macdonald; Hon. J. E. Michaud; Hon. C. D. Howe; Hon. L. S. St. Laurent.

Howe and his team soon got to work. They were housed in what was known as Number One Temporary Building, on Parliament Hill overlooking the Ottawa River. These ramshackle, clapboard buildings were put up during the war to meet a shortage of office space, although the word "temporary" proved to be a misnomer — they were not finally pulled down until 1978. Howe loved the building; its sparse furnishing and bleak functional appearance appealed to his no-nonsense approach, and he was to stay there for the rest of his political career.

His style of administration was refreshing to these businessmen, and a pleasant change from that of the dull, cautious Ottawa bureaucrats. Howe believed in delegating responsibility. Once he had picked a man for an important post — president of Trans-Canada Airlines, for example — he expected him to go away and get on with the job. "Keep out of here and keep out of trouble," he would say, "but if you're in deep, tell me."

An employee of Defence Industries Limited presents the 100 000 000th projectile produced in Canada — a heavy artillery shell — to C. D. Howe, Minister of Munitions and Supply.

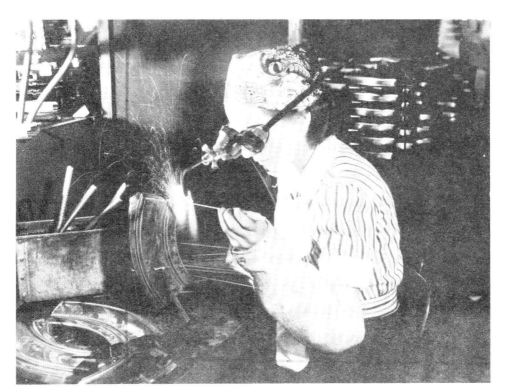

Like Sir Winston Churchill, Howe could not abide lengthy memoranda; he thought everything worth saying should be capable of being contained on a single sheet of paper. Even better, business could be conducted swiftly and efficiently on the phone, over a good lunch at the Rideau Club, or even on the golf course.

While Howe was finding the executives to work with him in government, he was also devising ways of mobilizing Canada's raw materials for war, to transform them into guns, shells, warships and aircraft. To do this, he returned to the crown corporation formula which he had used before the war to create Trans-Canada Airlines and the CBC.

The wartime crown corporations were managed by the executives Howe had gathered around him. This meant that they were operated like private companies, using the management methods of industry. The products they made included prefabricated sidings for barracks, nylon and kapok life preservers, parachutes, radar sets, fire control equipment and machine tools.

As part of the war effort, women were called upon to do many jobs formerly done only by men. For example, after a two-week high school course, this eighteen-year-old girl is welding Bren Gun magazines.

Within the DMS many of the executives were appointed as "controllers" to coordinate the production and distribution of all of Canada's domestic and imported raw materials, which were needed by both private companies and by the crown corporations.

Having set up the organization, Howe, like any good businessman, decided to pay a visit to his customers — in this case the British War Office. So when Parliament adjourned for Christmas early in December 1940, he prepared to sail for England. He took with him E.P. Taylor, W.C. Woodward and his deputy minister, Gordon Scott.

The four of them sailed from New York on December 6 on the *Western Prince*. This was no light-hearted undertaking. Crossing the Atlantic in winter at the best of times was hardly a pleasure cruise; and this wasn't the best of times. German submarines had the run of the Atlantic, using as bases the French ports that had been captured by Hitler's army when France fell in June, 1940. Hitler's policy was to blockade Britain, to prevent as much food and war material as possible from reaching the embattled island from its Canadian and American allies. So by the winter of 1940 the Atlantic was a dangerous place. Although the United States was still officially neutral, all ships were liable to be torpedoed on sight by the German U-boats.

The Howe family was aware of the dangers. William, the eldest son, was already serving as a midshipman in the Royal Navy. Alice was concerned that her husband might have to take to the lifeboats in mid-Atlantic, so she insisted that C.D. be properly prepared. She packed a hand-knitted bulky sweater, the brightly coloured tuque William had worn as a student at Bishop's College in Quebec, and a flask of brandy. Howe took all these preparations in his stride. The day he set sail, he wrote to his daughter Elisabeth: "Will try to send you a photo to show what the well dressed man should wear while being rescued."

Little did he know that just over a week later his photograph would indeed be taken in those very circumstances. For on the cold grey dawn of December 14, some five hundred kilometres off the coast of Ireland, the *Western Prince* was torpedoed, and sank within minutes. Howe and his colleagues found themselves in

the lifeboats alone on the pitching Atlantic seas. At least, not quite alone. For a frightening moment, the German submarine surfaced behind them. "I thought of being machine gunned or having a trip to Germany," Howe recalled. But the Germans dived again, leaving thirty-five cold, sea-sick men afloat on the rough seas.

Luck was on their side. A merchant ship picked up the *Western Prince's* last SOS. Disobeying standing orders that merchantmen were not to expose themselves needlessly to go to the rescue of other ships in trouble, the captain turned back to answer the call. Eight hours after they had taken to the boats, Howe and his fellow survivors were rescued. Sadly, in trying to climb the ropes from the lifeboat to the ship, Gordon Scott was crushed by the lifeboat, fell into the sea and was drowned.

Howe, ever cool in adversity and ever precise in his language, was later asked if his life passed before him while he was on the water. "Not at all," he said, "I was too busy bailing!" But the newspaper correspondent of the *Manchester Guardian*, who was torpedoed with him, told a more sobering story after their rescue. Howe said to him that however long he might live, every hour would be on "borrowed time" from that day on.

Howe (centre) after his rescue from the torpedoed Western Prince, *wearing the tuque his son wore at Bishop's College School in Quebec*

On Howe's right stands the famous industrialist E. P. Taylor.

Having lost his luggage on the Western Prince, *Howe hurriedly bought himself a badly-fitting suit in Glasgow. After he wore it to Buckingham Palace, King George VI commented that Howe was the worst-dressed person he had ever seen at a royal reception.*

Chapter 7 **The Pipeline Dispute**

Long before the Second World War ended, Prime Minister King and his ministers began to plan for the postwar period. By August 1944, with the successful Allied invasion of France and the Soviet Army's breakthrough into eastern Germany, it was clear the war in Europe would soon be over.

When Mackenzie King appointed C.D. Howe Minister of Reconstruction, in October 1944, it looked as though Howe would continue, in the years after the war,

Western leaders gather at the Quebec Conference in 1943. From left to right: Prime Minister Mackenzie King, President Roosevelt and Prime Minister Churchill.

to be one of Canada's most powerful ministers. One of his House of Commons opponents was to later call him "Minister of Everything." Yet there were signs, if not easily noticed in the general excitement of winning the war and planning for the peace, that Howe's strong methods and what critics called his dictatorial style would eventually get him into trouble.

Mackenzie King definitely wanted his super-minister in charge of organizing Canada's economy when the guns stopped. But King's concerns in the postwar period were different from Howe's. The Prime Minister was anxious to hold on to political power, and intended to put together a program of social service benefits and reforms, designed to convince the voters that under the Liberals the country would have better times than they had had before the war.

Mackenzie King held the office of Prime Minister for longer than anyone else in the British Commonwealth. He is shown here with his last cabinet, formed after the 1945 election. Howe is seated, third from left. Louis St. Laurent, the future Prime Minister, is seated at extreme left.

One Conservative opponent called Howe "a fascist- but a nice fascist!" What political party do you think Howe would be affiliated with today?

This policy helped King win the election in June 1945 — his last election. Howe, on the other hand, was out of sympathy with many of his cabinet colleagues when it came to social legislation. He was heard to remark to one reporter just after the end of the war that family allowances, a major program of the King government, "tend to encourage idleness and thus defeat our objective of maintaining production at its present level."

Along with his portfolio for Reconstruction and Supply, Howe was also appointed Minister of Trade and Commerce and, in April 1951, Minister of Defence Production. This was another new department formed to meet the familiar needs for weapons production, this time for the Korean War of 1950-53. As Defence Production Minister Howe maintained a strong personal role in the creation and management of Canada's postwar defence industries. But more than ever before, he ran into trouble in Parliament when he tried to hold on to the strong powers given during a wartime emergency which no longer existed.

Nevertheless, his power in Ottawa was substantial, and many suppliants came to his door. With the years, Howe's methods of working did not change. He still held court at Number One Temporary Building — broiling hot in summer, drafty and chill in winter. And summer or winter, C.D. would be at his desk by nine every morning. One of his staff recalled that "C.D. would be fresh in the morning, fresh as a daisy, when the rest of us felt like hell."

The first hour of his day was usually spent on departmental briefings. He expected precise assessments on current problems and programs, and committed a good deal of material to memory. He would be willing to forgive any member of his staff one mistake; but after a second blunder, the culprit rarely survived to make a third.

With his equals, the men who ran the great business and industrial enterprises of the nation, Howe's relations were frank and easy. They respected Howe as a tough-minded but fair man; he, in turn, had a flair for discovering executive talent, and once his trust was given, he could be relied upon to back up his friends.

Yet Howe had few intimate friends even among men he had worked with for years. When Howe left after his

brief stint as Minister of Reconstruction, private letters
of tribute flowed into his office from the big businessmen. Yet only one of the preserved letters was addressed
to him as "Clarence" and only a small handful as "C.D."
The writer who "dared" to call him Clarence was the
gruff and tough Donald Gordon, chairman of the
Wartime Prices and Trade Board and later president of
the CNR.

*Nowadays, fewer major
decisions are made by ministers
and more use is made of
committees. Do you think it
would be possible — or desirable
— for someone like C.D. Howe to
come to power today?*

In a time when successive Liberal governments in
Ottawa have practised patronage as openly as it was
used in the nineteenth century, C.D. Howe, who
personally appointed more prominent men to government jobs than any other cabinet minister in our history,
never once chose an executive or a public servant on the
basis of favouritism or to repay a political favour.

Mackenzie King retired in 1948, old and sick, to die in
1950. He was succeeded by the affluent and managerial
Louis St. Laurent, a former lawyer from Quebec City. He
and Howe got on well together, and Howe remained in
the St. Laurent cabinet. Both men preferred to run the
government of Canada as though it was a private
corporation or, as one parliamentary critic put it, "in a
tidy manner."

In the early 1950s Howe was still Minister of Trade
and Commerce and Minister of Defence Production,
conducting business as though the war was still going
on and assuming that his expedient methods of bypass-
ing red tape would be overlooked. As late as 1955, a
decade after the end of the war, he was still responsible
for twelve crown corporations, among them the Canadian
Wheat Board, Atomic Energy of Canada, Eldorado
Mining and, of course, his favourite, Trans-Canada
Airlines. Small wonder that Howe's political opponents
were becoming more vocal in their attacks on him for his
abuse of personal power.

One of these personal attacks resulted in the best-
remembered quote from Howe's long career in public
life. It has been often repeated as an example of his
supreme arrogance — the cynical remark, "What's a
million?" Except that Howe never made that remark.

In early 1946 the House of Commons was asked to
approve the last major estimate of more than one million
dollars for the Department of Munitions and Supply.
Howe was replying to a question on the amount from the

persistent J.M. Macdonnell, who was the Conservative party's financial critic. Howe commented: "I dare say my honourable friend could cut a million dollars from this amount. But a million dollars from the War Appropriations Bill would not be a very important matter."

John Diefenbaker, newly elected to Parliament in 1940, had scrapped with Howe from his first arrival in

After the war, Howe continued to be responsible for the production of armaments. One of his major projects was the development and production, during the 1950s, of the CF-100, an all-weather jet interceptor fighter. The CF-100s were built by A. V. Roe Canada Limited, under the close supervision of Howe's department.

Howe's special powers as defence production minister caused a stir in Parliament. The Opposition Leader, George Drew called them "the full mechanism of dictatorship." Again, Howe was in effect authorized to by-pass red tape in order to get things done quickly. In wartime, this practice had been accepted by Parliament as an unfortunate necessity; now it was seen as arrogant and undemocratic.

the House, and took part in the debate the next day by misquoting Howe as having said, "We may save a million dollars, but what of that?" From there the phrase "What's a million?" entered the permanent record of famous Canadian political sayings and there it has remained.

In the spring of 1956 Howe was seventy and had been in politics continuously for almost twenty-one

years. Every day of that time he had served as a federal cabinet minister wielding great power either bestowed on him or developed by him in office. But a year later, in the surprise electoral defeat of the Liberal Government in June 1957, he would be swept from office, never to return.

To explain how it all happened, we must go back to the late 1940s. At that time, the oil and natural gas boom in Alberta was just starting. With the discovery of the Leduc oil well in 1947, the attention of North America was drawn to the Canadian West as a plentiful source of cheap energy. Both American and Canadian promoters rushed in with schemes to transport the natural gas to the large urban centres of eastern Canada and the United States. The Albertans were cautious; until they knew the extent of their bonanza, they were wary about selling their birthright.

It is not surprising, therefore, that the government of Alberta was unwilling to give any private company the

The first Canadian designed and built all-weather fighter jet, the famous CF-100, is inspected by C.D. Howe, Defence Production Minister. With him, left to right, are Crawford Gordon, president of A.V. Roe Canada, Air Marshal Wilfrid Curtis, Chief of Air Staff, and Roy Dobson, Chairman of Hawker Siddeley, A.V. Roe's parent company.

Howe was also partly responsible for the initiation of Canada's nuclear power development plan. Here he turns the first sod of the Nuclear Power Demonstration Plant, Des Joachims, Ontario, on September 19, 1956.

right to export one of the province's greatest assets. By 1955, however, there were two main companies vying for permission to build a pipeline from Alberta to Toronto, Montreal and the eastern United States: they were Western Pipe Lines, a largely Canadian-owned company; and Trans-Canada Pipelines, a Canadian subsidiary of an American company.

Howe had kept a watching brief on the situation for some time. The head of Trans-Canada was a burly Texan, Clint Murchison. He and Howe got on well together: they were both dynamic, given to thinking big and taking risks. Gradually Howe became obsessed with the idea of an all-Canadian route for the pipeline, with no loops taking it down to supply the United States. This would be his last, and most exciting project — something that he saw as comparable to the building of the Canadian Pacific Railway in the nineteenth century, a massive construction and engineering feat that would boost the Canadian economy for years to come.

Howe said, "I believe this is a project that will make my children proud their father had a hand in it."

Howe started to sell his idea to the cabinet. Certainly those members from the East realized that Ontario, if it was to grow economically, would need an abundant supply of cheap energy, and were interested in Howe's idea. So the cabinet agreed to support Howe if he could find one company capable of building a transcontinental pipeline, and provided it ran straight across to eastern Canada, crossing only Canadian territory. Although most of the natural gas would be sold in Canada, to make the project feasible the cabinet realized some would have to be exported to the United States as well.

Howe got to work. He summoned the two competing companies to Ottawa in January 1954, and by a mixture of bullying and charm, he persuaded them to join together into one company, Trans-Canada Pipelines, to build the line. Although many Canadian businessmen were involved as directors on the board of this company, financial control was firmly in the hands of the Americans.

Trans-Canada now started to get the project off the ground. There were a great many things to be considered, and they all had to be made to fit together like pieces in a jigsaw puzzle. Contracts had to be negotiated with the construction companies who would actually build the line, with the oil companies who would supply the gas, and with the Canadian and American consumers who would buy it. To start construction Trans-Canada had to raise a large loan. But until some customers had agreed to buy the gas, no investors were interested in putting up their money; and until some of the pipeline was built, no consumers were willing to commit themselves to buying the gas. So — no money, no pipeline. It was a vicious circle, and Trans-Canada applied to Howe for help. Would the government be willing to guarantee the loan? With the Government of Canada behind them, investors would come forward.

Howe took the idea to the cabinet, and was met with a flat refusal. His colleagues were becoming aware that public criticism was rising over the involvement of American interests in selling Canada's gas. They were uneasy that such vital decisions affecting their country might be made in the boardrooms of New York and

Howe was always glad to see close ties between Canada and the United States. In the mid-fifties, he and Prime Minister St. Laurent (second from right) met with U.S. President Eisenhower (second from left) and Henry Cabot Lodge.

Texas. For the government to go a step further and actually put public money into an American-dominated company would be political dynamite.

Howe took this rebuff badly. The pipeline had become his consuming passion. Grumbling that he was part of "a government which has fallen into the hands of children," he desperately searched for some way to save his beloved project.

In the end it was Mitchell Sharp, his deputy minister at trade and commerce, who came up with the solution. The federal government and the government of Ontario would build the most costly part of the line across the Precambrian Shield of northern Ontario at their own expense. When the pipeline was in operation and making money, they would sell this part to Trans-Canada Pipelines, and get their investment back. Ontario agreed to the idea, and the project was back on track.

But by March 1956 another hitch had occurred. The U.S. government had not yet given their approval for American consumer companies to import Canadian natural gas, and until they did, Trans-Canada still couldn't raise enough money to build all of their part of the line. There was no doubt about this approval eventually being given, but it would mean that until it came there would be no money to send the work crews out into the field before the fall freeze-up on the prairies. Therefore, there would have to be a year's delay.

Looking back, it is difficult to understand Howe's frantic sense of urgency. Had he been willing to accept a year's delay, he might have avoided all the bitterness of the parliamentary debate that followed, and his own ignominious defeat. Was he, at seventy, even more conscious that he was living on "borrowed time"? Whatever the reason, a year's delay to him was unthinkable. He persuaded his cabinet colleagues to advance Trans-Canada the money they needed — a cool $80 million.

This was the substance of the bill that Howe eventually presented to Parliament on May 8, 1956. The government knew that the legislation would have to be passed by June 6, to get construction started. The Opposition knew this too. Aware of the widespread public apprehension over American involvement in the project, Conservative and CCF members joined together to prolong the debate and obstruct the passage of the bill by every available parliamentary device. By May 14 the bill had got nowhere, and time was running out. Howe made an impassioned speech in support of the pipeline. He tried to reassure his critics:

> The line will be built wholly within Canadian territory . . . the entire project is subject to Canadian law . . . not a cubic foot of gas can be exported to the United States without a permit from the Canadian government. In other words, whoever may own it, it is completely under Canadian control.

Still the Opposition criticism went on. In exasperation Howe told the House: "It is obvious that some Honourable Members prefer to obstruct this motion rather than debate it." Then he picked up a piece of paper from his desk and read these ominous words: "I beg to give notice that at the next sitting of Committee I shall move that further consideration of this resolution shall be the first business of the Committee and shall not further be postponed."

Pandemonium broke out on the Opposition benches. These words meant that their right to debate the issue was going to be strictly limited — in other words, closure. Under this rule, each member would only be allowed to speak for twenty minutes on each stage of the bill, instead of as often and for as long as he liked — or was able to stand on his feet.

The Opposition fought every stage of the bill tooth and nail, under the inspired leadership of the CCF member for Winnipeg, Stanley Knowles. During the acrimonious debate that followed, closure was imposed four times and fifty-three votes were taken to push the bill through in fifteen sitting days. Parliament was turned into a mad house — a scene of angry, confused and shouting members. When Donald Fleming, the Tory member from North Toronto, was suspended for a day for unparliamentary behaviour, a fellow Conservative draped a Union Jack over his empty desk. He was greeted at Toronto's Union Station by cheering supporters also waving Union Jacks as though he was a war hero.

Prime Minister St. Laurent sat silent and expressionless through most of the bitter debate, making no move in public to support Howe until May 31, when he rose to move final closure to get the bill through the second last

In an official ceremony at the border of Canada and the United States, C. D. Howe joined the pipeline connecting an oil tanker terminal in Portland, Maine, with refineries in Montreal, Quebec.

stage of the House of Commons voting procedure. As for Howe himself, he made the supreme comment of the day and of the stormy event which suggested he was now beyond any personal reconciliation with changing times when he admitted to a Liberal colleague: "I was never so bored in all my life."

Amid scenes of unprecedented disorder, the Trans-Canada Pipeline Bill won final parliamentary passage on June 2, 1956, and royal assent four days later. The following day, June 7, Trans-Canada work crews started to lay the pipelines across the prairies.

Prime Minister St. Laurent

Chapter 8 The End of an Era

C.D. Howe inspects another Canada-U.S. project, the DEW line (Distant Early Warning), a chain of radar stations built in Canada and maintained in cooperation with U.S. technicians, to detect the approach of hostile aircraft.

When the battle was over, Parliament recessed for the summer, and the politicians went home to lick their wounds and take the pulse of the electorate. Howe himself was, as usual, supremely confident. "I doubt if the sudden application of closure made much difference in the long run. Both the Tories and the CCF had announced that they intended to block passage of the bill, and we were working against the deadline. The main thing is the pipeline is now under construction . . . I think that this ground can be regained in time. It looks to me as if we will be net gainers by next June."

In one way he was right. After passage of the bill customers flocked to sign contracts to buy the gas, investors rushed to put money into Trans-Canada Pipelines, and the company repaid the government loan by February 1957. Natural gas would flow to Toronto and Montreal by 1958. Had the bill been defeated, Canadian gas would eventually have gone south to the United States. Howe used American money and expertise to guarantee Canadian gas for Canadian consumers.

But in another way Howe was desperately wrong. To the electorate, the argument was not over who should build or finance the pipeline so much as over government arrogance and total disregard for Parliament. The use of closure was seen as a culmination of years of Liberal dictatorship — and the dictator-in-chief was, of course, C.D. Howe.

Howe did not understand this. In his mind, the cabinet was like the board of directors of a large corporation. They knew what was good for the country; occasionally the shareholders — the electorate — could give the directors' decisions a vote of confidence in an election. Apart from that, Howe thought the public should be content to leave the government to run the country without interference.

In the election of June 1957 the Liberal party were to find how far from the truth this view was. An aroused electorate threw the St. Laurent government out, and replaced it with a minority Conservative government led by the man who had fought against Liberal arrogance in the pipeline debate and who claimed to speak to the ordinary people of Canada — John George Diefenbaker.

When the votes were counted, half the Liberal cabinet had been defeated and among them, unbelievably, was the all-powerful C.D. Howe. In his riding of Port Arthur, he had been soundly beaten by an unknown local school teacher, Douglas Fisher, running for the CCF.

The election campaign at the Lakehead told the story. Fisher took his case to the people. The CCF bought time on the local television station, and their candidate appeared night after night, to explain about Liberal arrogance and the need for new ideas made in Canada, and younger leaders. When Howe belatedly appealed to his riding, he presented the picture of an irritable, tired old man, out of touch with the mood of the voters.

The result was decisive: Fisher won the seat by over one thousand votes, and C.D. Howe's career was over.

Howe was never one for recriminations. After the initial shock was over, he accepted his defeat with dignity. A few days later he returned to Ottawa and gathered up his few private papers from his modest office. He and Alice bought a house in Montreal and left the Ottawa scene for good. Howe's parting comment about the new Conservative government was characteristically brief and caustic: "I don't trust this new bunch very much."

C.D. Howe's last few years were quiet and out of the public eye. He assumed directorships in about a dozen corporations at the invitation of his business friends. He accepted the chancellorship of his old university, Dalhousie, an appointment that gave him particular pleasure. He spent more time with his wife and family than he had been able to do for decades. He and Alice had bought a country house in St. Andrews, New Brunswick, in 1952, and now they could spend more time there, surrounded by their grandchildren.

But Howe was not one to sit around doing nothing, even in his old age. To the end, he was constantly travelling across the country (often on "his" airline) attending board meetings, receiving honorary degrees, advising his business friends. It was a killing pace, and inevitably his health gave way. On New Year's Eve in 1959, C.D. Howe died quietly of a heart attack at his home in Montreal.

In some ways he had outlived his time. His managerial style of government was out of fashion. New men and women and new ideas were coming to the fore in the Liberal party: the diplomat Lester Pearson with his preference for the conciliator's approach; and later, the aristocratic, intellectual Pierre Trudeau, to whom so often style seemed more important than substance. Howe had nothing in common with such men. He brought to the practice of politics his engineer's common sense and a businessman's ability to take quick decisions and make them stick. His only criterion on any project was: Does it work? If so, let's go ahead and do it. Parliamentary niceties irritated him, and in his later years he increasingly tried to operate outside parliamen-

The Right Honourable C. D. Howe

His greatest legacy was his confidence in Canada's industrial potential. "Never again," he said, "will there be any doubt that Canada can manufacture anything that can be manufactured elsewhere."

tary approval. As one of his most vigorous opponents, Stanley Knowles, put it: "Parliament got in his way."

But Howe's legacy lives on. The era of prosperity and industrial progress that he master-minded after the Second World War has given Canada one of the highest standards of living in the world. More than that, this great American-born Canadian who is so often blamed for the foreign domination of our resources, built for us a Canadian communications system. But for him, there would have been no national transcontinental air service, no national broadcasting system, no all-Canadian natural gas pipeline. When so much of our trade flows from north to south across the border with the United States, we should remember the strong-minded, stubborn politician who believed that it should also go from east to west, from one coast of Canada to the other.

Further Reading

Ashley, C.A. and Smails, R.G. *Canadian Crown Corporations. Some Aspects of their Administration and Control.* Toronto: Macmillan Company of Canada, 1965.

Bothwell, R. and Kilbourn, W. *C.D. Howe: A Biography.* Toronto: McClelland and Stewart Limited, 1979.

Granatstein, J.L. *W.L. Mackenzie King.* Toronto: Fitzhenry & Whiteside Limited, 1976.

Hayes, W.A. *Beaverbrook.* Toronto: Fitzhenry & Whiteside Limited, 1979.

Howe, C.D. *Industry and Government in Canada.* Meisel Lecture to the Chemical Industry Society, London, England, published in *Chemistry and Industry*, 1958.

Roberts, L. *The Life and Times of Clarence Decatur Howe.* Toronto: Clarke, Irwin & Company Limited, 1957.

Credits

The author and publishers are grateful to James Dodge (C.D.Howe's son-in-law), William Howe (his son) and Stanley Howe (his nephew), for their assistance during research for this book; also to the Honourable Mitchell Sharp; and to the following, who permitted the use of copyright material:

Harbron, John, pages 7, 9, 11, 17, 18, 35, 53.
International Press, page 13
London Daily Mail, page 45
Manitoba Archives, pages 20-21
Provincial Archives of Canada, pages 4-5 (472), 14(C-85854), 23(C-20113), 25(C-9076), 26(C-30305), 29(C-79597), 31(C-19380), 34(C-63377), 39(C-55372), 41(C-26922), 42(C-7487), 43(C-75212), 46(C-14168), 47(C-26988), 55(C-53459), 58(C-7485), title page (C-68669), 63 and cover (C-5337).
Royal Canadian Navy, page 38.

Every effort has been made to credit all sources correctly. The author and publishers will welcome   information that would allow them to correct any errors or omissions.

Index